FRIENDS *of* RICHMOND PARK *Family Trails in*

RICHMOND PARK

First published in 2011 by The Friends of Richmond Park
www.frp.org.uk
Registered charity number 1133201

© The Friends of Richmond Park, 2011

ISBN 978-0-9567469-1-7

All text and photographs by Susanna Ramsey

Edited by Teresa Grafton and Ron Crompton

Design and production by Alison Graham
The London Design Factory Ltd
design.factory@btinternet.com
020 8332 2432

Printed by Unity Print and Publishing
www.unity-publishing.co.uk
020 8487 2199

Introduction

I have lived close to Richmond Park for more than twenty years and walk there almost every day. It is a source of enormous joy, comfort and inspiration to me and I love every part of it. It is familiar but always changing, with the weather, seasons and time of day.

There are the cold, frosty mornings and warm summer evenings; days when the wind blows through the long grass, filled with butterflies, and skylarks are singing in the sky; times when the autumn leaves stack up beneath your feet, stags bellow and fungi appear out of nowhere; and sultry hours to hunt for dragonflies at the water's edge and watch the swifts and swallows flying over Pen Ponds.

Walking and particularly walking slowly is the way to discover the Park and its wildlife. You see, hear and smell nature in a way that you would never experience running, cycling or even striding out. These trails take you to places in the Park where you can fully use your senses to experience its nature.

I first created these trails for my daughter Katie, when she was about nine, as a treasure hunt for her to do at the weekends. We have spent hours in the Park, walking with our dog Daisy, playing hide and seek, jumping ditches and taking photos. I hope these trails help you to enjoy the delights of the Park with your family as much as I have with mine.

Susanna Ramsey, June 2011

Acknowledgements

This book would not have come together without the help and contributions of a large number of people who kindly gave their time and work voluntarily. A very big thank you to Ron Crompton, Chairman of the Friends, who has supported and overseen this project from the outset; Teresa Grafton, the Friends' Education Officer, who tested out the trails with me, often in sub-zero temperatures, and edited the text with admirable patience; and Richard Gray, one of the Friends' Trustees, who conceived the idea of turning the set of trails into a book.

Thank you to everyone who provided valuable contributions to the trails, suggesting information to include and inspiring me with their own incredible knowledge of the Park: Peter Burrows- Smith, Tim Howard, John Karter, Max Lankester, Franko Maroevic, Steve Read, Jan Wilczur and Simon Richards, the Park Manager.

Thank you also to The Royal Parks for the use of the map of Richmond Park and to Alison Graham of The London Design Factory for designing and producing the book.

Important notes about the trails

These walks are intended to be discovery trails, which lead you off the beaten track to explore different areas of the Park, away from the tarmac and gravel paths. Most of the walks follow grassy paths or indistinct tracks. They are unlikely to be suitable for buggies.

The route will not always be totally clear as the appearance and accessibility of the paths changes with the seasons; sometimes the bracken is high and it can be difficult to see the way ahead. Sometimes you will have to find your own way through a wood or up a hill.

Some items listed in the walks, such as log piles or even trees, are not permanent structures and may disappear over time. Other items such as fungi and butterflies will only appear in their appropriate season. For these reasons, you are unlikely to see everything in each of the walks. If you cannot find an object, just continue with the walk and hope that you might find it on another occasion or see something similar on a different walk.

The walks are not signposted at all. Indeed there are very few signposts in the Park. You should not be surprised if you do not manage to follow the routes exactly. As long as you discover different areas of the Park, learn more about the diversity of its wildlife and find your way home without getting too lost, the walks will be enjoyable and each time you return your experiences of the Park will be richer.

Contents

Introduction and   3
Acknowledgements

Important notes about   4
the trails

Tread Lightly   6

Foreword   7
by Jacqueline Wilson

TRAIL ONE   9
Ps and Qs Walk

TRAIL TWO   19
Up and Down Walk

TRAIL THREE   31
Three Gates and
a Dark Hill Walk

TRAIL FOUR   43
See-Through Tree Walk

TRAIL FIVE   55
Distant Views Walk

TRAIL SIX   67
The Ponds Walk

The Nature Collection   77

Friends of Richmond Park 78

Richmond Park Facts   79

Useful Information   80

Inside back cover
Map of Richmond Park

Tread Lightly

Richmond Park is there for everyone to enjoy. But it is also a National Nature Reserve, with a fragile ecology. Please 'tread lightly' and help preserve this beautiful Park and its wildlife. As walkers we can do this by:

Wildlife

- Keeping to the established paths as far as possible. This avoids disturbing the wildlife and harming grassland, wild flowers and fungi.
- Not damaging anything. For example, do not jump on the ant hills (the young ants grow up in the domes). Imagine a giant jumping on your roof!
- Not climbing trees, moving dead or decaying wood (which is home to beetles), or picking anything (especially wild flowers and fungi, which could be poisonous).
- Not building shelters out of dead branches and twigs. These could collapse on people and hurt them. Also, beetles and invertebrates living in the dead wood will be destroyed.
- Taking nothing away from the Park. This includes any fungi, mushrooms deer antlers, sweet chestnuts, grasses and flowers. They all provide food for wildlife and some grasses and flowers are specially protected.
- Not dropping litter or leaving food behind. Human food is hard for deer to digest and some have died from indigestible litter clogging their stomach.
- Not feeding the ducks, swans and other wild birds. Bread is not part of their natural diet.
- Not lighting any fires or barbecues at any time.

Dogs

- Respecting the 'Dogs on Leads" signs near the ponds where wildfowl breed (currently Pen, Adam's and Bishop's).
- Keeping dogs on leads in the skylark protection area, between the Lower Pen Pond and the car park, during the breeding season in spring and summer. Skylarks are ground nesting birds. They are easily disturbed and their eggs might get trampled on.
- Not taking dogs into Pembroke Lodge and Gardens (except guide dogs) and keeping dogs on leads in the Isabella Plantation.
- Controlling dogs near deer and not getting too close, particularly if there are young deer, when the females are likely to be very aggressive and may attack. During the autumn rut the male deer can be dangerous if approached.
- Cleaning up after your dogs. Their waste is rich in nutrients which damage the acid grassland.

This may seem a long list but we all need to respect and protect this very special environment, otherwise it could be changed forever. It is easy to cause damage without realising the impact we are having.

Foreword

I really love Richmond Park. I've been going for wonderful walks there ever since I was six years old. In fact my recent children's book 'Lily Alone' is actually set in Richmond Park and I have a chance to describe some of my favourite parts. Children who read it have said: "I can't believe there could be such a fabulous enormous wild place. Our park is boring. Are there really herds of deer there? Are there actually huge hollow oak trees? Are there lots of ponds and special gardens with masses of flowers?"

Richmond Park has all these delights - and many more. It's a wonderful haven for wildlife, just a few miles from central London. It's great for a day out.

This book will help you explore every corner of Richmond Park. Six very different trails lead you deep in to the Park, uncovering all kinds of secrets on the way.

The trails are easy to follow and packed with information about the Park. You'll find out about the deer and the oak trees, the birds and the butterflies, the historical buildings and the mysterious woods. You'll learn about nature in all its forms: turkey oak acorns, tiny gall wasps, stag beetles, tawny owls, great spotted woodpeckers, yellow meadow ants and birch polypore fungus.

You'll see how the landscape changes when you do each walk throughout the seasons. Each trail will turn you into a nature detective, following tracks to hunt down the next clue. A walk in the Park will never be the same again, and you'll know so much more about its wildlife and history.

I do hope you enjoy this book and learn to love Richmond Park as much as I do.

Jacqueline Wilson

Family Trail Number One

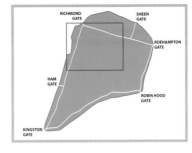

Ps and Qs Walk

A walk which leads you to Pen Ponds (the two Ps), the largest ponds in the centre of the Park. Follow a dark, winding track through an enclosed wood and emerge into Queen Elizabeth's Plantation (the first Q) of ancient oak trees. Explore the plantation, looking for acorns and fungi. Come out by a small pond with lovely open views across the Park in all directions. Walk down to Pen Ponds to enjoy the different ducks, geese and swans. Cross the broad tree-lined Queen's Ride (the second Q). Make your way back up the hill through a plantation of sweet chestnut trees. You might even spot some deer!

Distance: approximately 2 miles / 3 km.
Time: 1 to 2 hours (depending on pace).

Route: From Pembroke Lodge, through Sidmouth Wood to Queen Elizabeth's Plantation. Past Leg of Mutton Pond to Pen Ponds and up through Saw Pit Plantation.

From Pembroke Lodge car park, cross the road and walk straight ahead until you reach the fence in front of you. Turn left and keep going until you get to the black, iron kissing gate into Sidmouth Wood. Go through the gate and stay on the only available footpath, through the wood.

1. Sidmouth Wood is named after Lord Sidmouth, former Prime Minister and also the Park Ranger in the early 1800s. Tangled rhododendron plants make the entrance to this wood feel like a secret place. The rhododendron are gradually being removed and replaced with native tree species.

2. Birch Polypore Fungus. Look at the silver birch trees on the right when the path opens out. This cream brown fungus grows high up, out of the trunks. In the past, people used it as a firelighter, to sharpen cut-throat razors and to stop bleeding. Museums use strips for mounting insects such as butterflies.

*Come out into Queen Elizabeth's Plantation. Walk straight ahead through the wood, heading for the bottom left hand corner, where a path leads out to Pen Ponds. Aim for the silver birch tree with four trunks growing out of one base. To find **items 4 to 8** you need to spread out and explore the wood, hunting around on the ground. Most of these items only appear in autumn and winter.*

3. Ancient Oak Trees. There are over 40,000 oak trees in the Park. Some date back to the 14th century. An oak's age can be measured in hugs around its trunk. Each adult hug represents about 100 years, and a child hug about 75. Choose a tree to measure.

4. Turkey Oak Acorns. Can you find any acorn cups from the turkey oak trees on the ground? These are covered in shaggy bristles, unlike the cups from the English oak. The twigs have whiskers around the buds in winter. The turkey oak is not a native species. It was introduced from southern Europe.

5. Fungi. On the scattered dead tree trunks, look for different species of fungi. Also mosses and lichens. The fungus pictured here is jelly ear. You can see why! You might find other fungi here too: turkey tail, coral spot, fly agaric, candlewick, beefsteak and chicken of the woods.

6. Galls. Can you see any strange shapes on the ground beneath the oak trees? These are galls, created by tiny gall wasps, whose larvae grow inside the lumps. Pictured here is a knopper gall which forms around an acorn. Marble galls grow on twigs and are small, round and smooth.

7. Chestnuts (pictured here) provide a valuable food source for mammals, birds and insect larvae, all of which leave different feeding signs. Squirrels rip the shell apart, mice and voles gnaw a hole and birds and insect larvae leave small neat holes.

8. Woodpeckers. In spring, great spotted woodpeckers (pictured here) drum on the trees as they mark out their territory. Each year they make a new nest hole. The great spotted woodpecker is about as big as a blackbird. The much rarer lesser spotted woodpecker also lives in the Park. It looks similar to this one, but is about the size of a house sparrow. It stays up in the tree canopy and so is very hard to see. Green woodpeckers are the largest woodpeckers in the Park, being similar in size to a pigeon, but slimmer! They often fly up out of the open grassland, with a laughing call. All woodpeckers fly with a bouncing motion. They close their wings after a few flaps, rising and falling rather like a shallow wave (called undulating flight).

Find the four-trunked silver birch tree. Go to the silver birch tree on your left, which is arching out of the wood. Face the pond and look slightly back to your right to see item 9, about 10m away.

9. Pin Oak Tree scraped by Deer Antlers. The leaves on this tree have pins on the tips. The bark has been scratched by the antlers of dominant male deer during the autumn rut, to mark out their territory. In spring deer shed their antlers and grow new ones, often eating the old ones as a source of calcium. Antlers are a form of bone but feel more like wood. Other animals may also nibble the fallen antlers, which are rarely found by walkers.

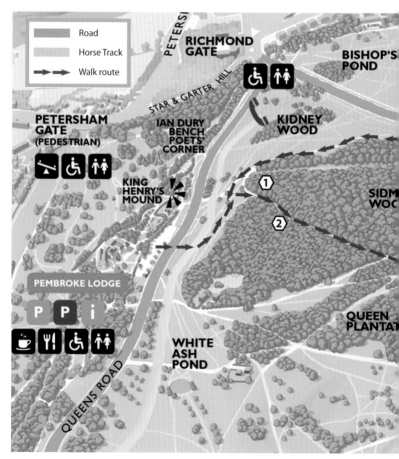

Cross the horse track and walk to Leg of Mutton Pond. Then walk beside the pond and continue along the path straight ahead to Pen Ponds.

10. Deer Prints, called Slots. Can you see any in the horse track? Red deer are the largest deer in the Park. Adult males can weigh up to 200kg. Fallow deer, which are paler brown and speckled, are much smaller, with males weighing up to 95 kg. Can you see different sized slots? Which way were they heading?

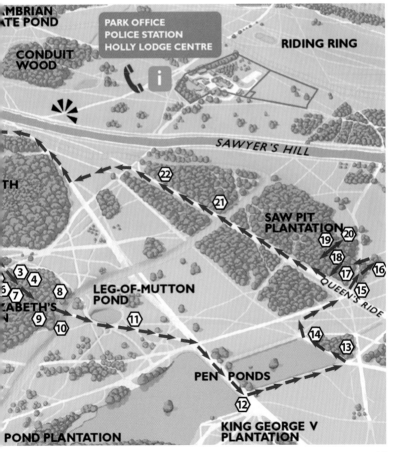

11. Leg of Mutton Pond. You can see from its shape how this pond got its name. It used to be called Pen Pond, but another name had to be found when the two large ponds nearby became known as Pen Ponds. It is one of the oldest ponds in the Park, dating back to 1637.

At Pen Ponds go along the path between the ponds. Turn left and left again around Lower Pen Pond, hugging the edge of the pond.

12. Water Birds. Swans live for up to 14 years and normally mate for life. They are the heaviest British bird, with males (cobs) weighing up to 15kg. The ones here are mute swans. They are less vocal than the other swan species, hence their name. Swans have up to 25,000 feathers. You may also see coots, which are black with white frontal (face) shields and bills, and the smaller moorhens, which are brownish-black with a white line on the side of their body and a red frontal shield above the yellow bill. Also look out for the glossy green-headed mallard drakes with curly tail feathers.

13. Folded Willow Tree. This looks as if it has been folded up! There are often birds in the willow trees here: goldfinches, blue tits and parakeets. Look too, for herons standing at the edge of the pond, or large, black cormorants diving for fish. In summer you might see damselflies or larger dragonfly species in the long grasses beside the pond. The common blue damselfly has sky blue and black stripes.

14. Parakeet Hole. This is almost at the end of the path. Go past the tree and look back to see the hole. It is the kind parakeets might nest in.

These birds are easy to see because they are bright green and very noisy! They have a long tail and crimson beak. Parakeets are an alien species rapidly growing in numbers. It is possible that they compete with native birds for food and nest-holes and may become an agricultural pest, like some geese.

When you reach the end of the pond, turn 90 degrees to your right, towards the road in the distance. Head for the bottom of the large wood which covers the hill over to your left. This is Saw Pit Plantation. Do not go into the plantation but walk on the open grass, just below it. Cross the broad, tree-lined avenue (Queen's Ride) leading up to White Lodge, which is hidden from view initially. Continue skirting the edge of the plantation until you reach the Feeding Manger (16), which is in a small group of trees.

15. Queen's Ride and White Lodge.
This avenue leads up, to your right, to White Lodge, home of the Royal Ballet School. It was built in 1727 as a hunting lodge, and later became the home of the Park's Ranger or Deputy Ranger. Lord Sidmouth lived here for over 40 years until he died in the Lodge in 1844.

In 1805 Lord Sidmouth entertained Lord Nelson here. It is said that Nelson dipped his finger in his wine glass to trace out on the dining table his battle plan for destroying the French fleet. Six weeks later he carried out this plan at the Battle of Trafalgar! The future King Edward VIII was born here in 1894.

16. Winter Feeding Manger for the Deer.
This is just below Saw Pit Plantation. There is not enough grazing for the deer in winter, so each night they are fed with hay, maize and deer pellets by the gamekeepers who work in the Park. Their job is to look after the deer and the rest of the wildlife.

Make your way through the wood to rejoin Queen's Ride.

17. Small Woodland Birds. At the bottom of the wood you might see small birds like the nuthatch (pictured here) or treecreeper, scuttling over the trunk and branches in a search for insects. The nuthatch is the only British bird which walks down a tree trunk head first. The mottled brown treecreeper often lands near the base of a tree and spirals up.

18. Jackdaws. These noisy black birds have black caps on grey heads. They are smaller than crows, which are all black. Jackdaws nest inside tree holes but crows nest in the branches. You can often see crows around the waste bins looking for food left by humans.

Walk up Queen's Ride away from White Lodge until you come to a single pine tree on your right, before the rhododendron patch. Here you have a choice. You can carry straight on up Queen's Ride to item 22, or take a detour back into the wood to look for items 19 to 21. For the detour, go from this pine tree straight back into the wood, looking for the trees in the next two pictures. The oak is a medium sized tree, half way into the wood, with branches which curl horizontally. The silver birch will be on your left just before you reach the oak.

19. Woodpecker Holes in the silver birch tree. There are several holes high up on the trunk. A woodpecker's toes are specially adapted to grip on to the bark of a tree while it is drumming. The tail feathers too are unusually stiff, to give extra support. You might spot a woodpecker by the way it approaches a tree, flying in to land vertically against the trunk.

20. Oak Tree with Curly Branches. The way the branches curl around is very rare. Oak trees can support hundreds of different species of invertebrates, such as moth larvae, gall wasps and beetles. Leaf litter provides food for all kinds of microscopic fungi and bacteria.

21. Deer. You will often see them in this wood. Although red deer are not speckled, their young (calves) are born with speckled coats which act as good camouflage. The young are mainly born in June and are often left hidden in the bracken and long grass by their mothers when they go off to feed. The mothers can be very protective and aggressive at this time so keep well away, especially if you see a solitary female. If you find a young fawn or calf, never touch it.

Deer shed their antlers in March and April each year. When the new antlers grow they are covered in velvet. This is rubbed off in time for the autumn rut, when the stags fight each other for dominance.

Come back out of the wood the way you went in and rejoin Queen's Ride, turning right. Walk up the broad avenue, towards the road and open grass.

22. Mortlake Parish Boundary Stone. Look out for this low square stone on your right, just before the end of Queen's Ride. It is close to the ninth tree down from the top of the avenue. The stone is dated 1857.

When you come out of Queen's Ride, bear left towards the railings around Sidmouth Wood. Keep the railings on your left and the road on your right. Slightly further on, look back across the road for views of the city of London. Follow the railings round to your left. When you are level with Pembroke Lodge car park, cross the road.

Family Trail Number Two

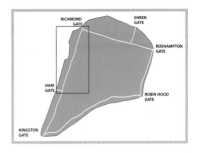

Up and Down Walk

A very hilly walk! Set off through a tree-lined avenue and continue along the top of a hill, enjoying views over Kingston . Go down the hill and walk beside the polo field, a popular place for picnics and games. Climb back up to join a grassy track towards Richmond, looking out over the open grassland, planted with cedars and pines. Walk down the steep hill beneath the oak and plane trees to the children's playground at Petersham Gate. Then climb the hill again to Pembroke Lodge.

Distance: approximately 2 miles / 3 km. Time: 1.5 to 2 hours (depending on pace).

Route: From Pembroke Lodge car park to Ham Gate Pond, then beside the Polo Field and back towards Pembroke Lodge. Along the top of the hill below Pembroke Lodge gardens, down to Petersham Gate and back to Pembroke Lodge.

Start the walk outside the Visitor Centre. With Pembroke Lodge behind you, turn right and walk alongside the railings out of the car park. Stay on top of the hill and when the railings curve round to the right, keep straight ahead and walk on the footpath, not the shared cycle/pedestrian path which is closer to the road. After admiring the view to your right, carry on to the avenue of hornbeams.

1. Hornbeam Avenue. Hornbeams are native British trees which have a smooth grey/green bark and oval, pointed leaves. This avenue of hornbeams was planted in the 1840s. The older hornbeams (down the hill to your right) have folds and little holes in the trunk, which collect pools of rainwater. These pools are an ideal habitat for tiny invertebrates.

Hornbeams were traditionally pollarded, or chopped off, at shoulder height. This caused new branches to shoot out, producing extra timber that could be used for mill wheels, piano hammers or firewood.

2. Tree Identity Tags. Several trees in the avenue have a round or oblong metal tag. This indicates that they are veteran trees - that is, ones which because of age, size or condition are considered to be of exceptional value. All the veteran trees in the Park are listed. The list is also part of a national register of ancient trees (compiled by the Ancient Tree Hunt).

At the end of Hornbeam Avenue, just before the little bridge across a stream, turn right to see the huge oak (item 3). Join the path further from the road.

3. Huge Oak. (The photo shows the tree from a different angle). There are about 600 different types of oak tree in the world. A mature oak produces 25,000 leaves each year. Nearly 300 different species of insect can live on mature oak trees.

Each oak tree provides a range of mini habitats for birds, insects, tiny invertebrates and fungi. These include sunny branches covered in leaves, thick bark, dark cracks behind the bark, cavities inside the trunk, dead wood and leaf litter below the tree. Each is the perfect environment for certain species of wildlife, from woodpeckers and bluetits, to caterpillars and stag beetles. What wildlife can you see?

4. Hawthorn Trees around a little pond. (On the left, immediately after the oak). Woods may have different levels of vegetation: the canopy at the top, the understorey (made up of shorter trees like the hawthorn) the

field layer (bracken and grasses) and the ground layer. The hawthorns are important because they provide vegetation and shelter for birds and insects at the understorey level. They also provide nectar for invertebrates and berries (pictured previous page) for birds in winter. Look for frogspawn in the pond in spring and damselflies in the summer.

5. Horse Chestnut (Conker) Trees. About 300m after the pond, when you have been over the little hill, look out for a group of trees off to the left of the path. These trees have an extensive root system above the ground. The roots are covered in moss and lichen and have little circular knobs and pools on them.

Look on the ground for a twig from the horse chestnut tree. When the leaves fall off in the autumn, they leave a scar on the twig, shaped like a horse shoe. In winter look up at the large, sticky leaf buds on the ends of the twigs. In spring the trees are covered in blossom which provides nectar for bees and other insects.

6. Base of an old Oak Tree. You will find this at the very end of the top path. Several of the oak trees in the Park are 600 years old and would have been here at the time of the Great Fire of London and the Plague. Look at the beautiful detail and texture of the bark. So many shades of brown!

Turn right and go down the hill to Ham Gate Pond.

7. Ham Gate Pond appears on a map of the Park, dated 1754. It is one of the oldest ponds in the Park, where you might see mallards, rainbow coloured mandarin ducks or Egyptian geese. The last two species nest in tree holes. As soon as the young have hatched, they have to fall out of the tree hole and follow the adults to the nearest water.

Often there are broods of young ducklings in the summer as well as a family of Egyptian geese, which stay together for weeks, and sometimes months, before the young are fully independent. The goslings take a long time to grow their adult feathers. You might also see a large grey heron perched in a tree at the back of the pond or spot a terrapin in the water. There are toilets at Ham Gate and a drinking water fountain.

8. Alder Trees grow beside this pond. The female catkins look like small cones. They start off purple, turn green in the summer, then darken and stay on the tree until the following spring. The seeds have an oily coating so that they can be distributed by the water.

In winter flocks of birds such as siskins, redpolls or goldfinches feed on the alder seeds. Siskins have a streaky yellow/green body and a black crown. Redpolls are predominately streaky brown above and white below; the male has a red forehead. Goldfinches have a sandy brown and white body, black wings with a yellow wing bar and a red face.

Turn right along the shared path towards Petersham. At the end of the polo field, bear right up the hill and walk past two fence barriers. Just before you get to the top of the hill, head for the bench, below another, much longer, fence barrier. Walk along the indistinct path, which runs below Pembroke Lodge gardens. (This is part of the Capital Ring walk). Keep the railings on your right. Keep going along the top path.

9. Two Fir Trees, tied together. These trees inside Pembroke Lodge gardens are strapped together, to prevent them falling over! These gardens were laid out 150 years ago and are well worth a visit. Features include the dell area with specimen trees and winding paths; areas laid out with formal bedding; a rose garden and a magnificent laburnum arch, at its best in May. There is a gate on your right here, which leads into the gardens.

Unless you have a dog with you, you can enter and go in to the café for some refreshments or sit on the terrace, enjoying the panoramic views towards Kingston and the Thames Valley.

10. Pembroke Lodge. On this path is a good place to admire this beautiful white Georgian mansion with stepped gabling. Lord John Russell lived at the Lodge when he was Prime Minister from 1847 onward and many cabinet meetings were held here. His grandson, the famous philosopher, Bertrand Russell, grew up here.

11. Coronet Pruning. If you look down the hill on your left, there is a tree where the branches have been pruned to look like crowns. These spiky points imitate the way a branch would break off naturally. This encourages fungi to grow on the tree, which will rot away the dead wood at the centre. Beefsteak fungus (pictured here) is wide-spread in the Park. Dead trees with hollow cavities are very important

habitats for fungi, beetles, bats and birds. The decaying wood is an important food source for a wide range of insects such as beetles. Birds and bats feed on these insects and their larvae.

Road

Horse Track

Walk route

PETER

HAM GATE POND

7

8

HAM DIP POND

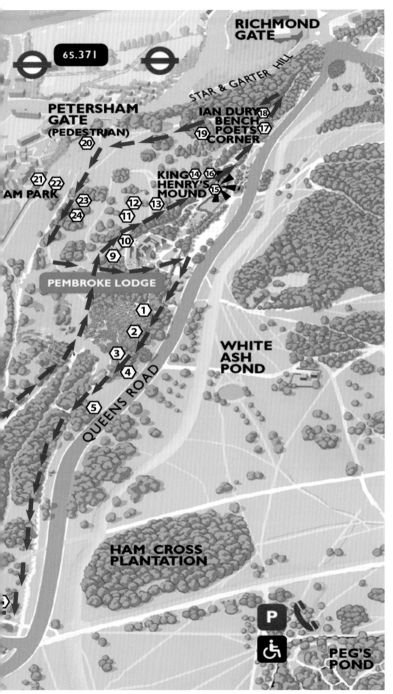

12. Sequoia Tree. This is the tall pyramid shaped conifer, half way down the hill. There are only a few sequoias in the Park. The sequoia is native to the western USA, where they grow to incredible heights and can weigh more than 6,000 tonnes! Sequoias were introduced to Britain in the 19th century. The small, female cones are about 8cm long. They are dark brown, deeply fissured and feel like cork. The bark of the sequoia has evolved to resist forest fires and chars to form a protective heat shield when burnt.

13. Fallen Tree. (On your right, just after another gate into Pembroke Lodge gardens.) This trunk looks like a pair of legs! Can you see any fungi on the trunk? Sometimes there is a brown fungus called jelly ear fungus (pictured here). It looks like a rash of ears on the trunk!

On a clear day, there are great views at this point to your left. You can see Ham House and the planes going in and out of Heathrow airport. You might even see Windsor Castle.

Keep walking along the track at the top of the hill. Ignore the sign for the Capital Ring walk, which leads down the slope.

14. Ant Hills. The bumps in the grass are ant hills, not mole hills. (There are no longer any moles in the Park). The hills have been made by the yellow meadow ants, and each mound is many decades, if not centuries, old. Queen ants living inside some of these hills can live for more than 20 years! Please be careful not to damage them.

Green woodpeckers (pictured) feed on the ants and fly up out of the grass here. These woodpeckers have a red crown and a yellow rump above their tail. They fly low, with a swooping, wave-like action, a few flaps and then a glide. Listen for their laughing call.

15. Small Domed Building. This brick house was built to cover a reservoir which extends three metres below the ground. It collects water from springs in the grounds of Pembroke Lodge and used to send it down a tunnel to supply the Russell School (see item 20).

16. Fallen Lime Tree with most of the roots exposed. This tree was blown over in the 1987 hurricane and the branches have formed new trees, growing out of its side. These are known as phoenix trees. It shows how a tree can survive and thrive despite such a natural disaster.

17. Birch Polypore. You may see this cream shelf-like fungus on the silver birch trees, in the pile of jumbled branches, next to the fence around Pembroke Lodge gardens. Mind the stinging nettles!

Keep going along the path, almost to the end.

18. Pile of tree stumps, which have been sawn through. If you look at the tree stumps, you will see patterns of rings, usually one light then one dark. By counting the rings you can estimate the age of the tree. (These stumps are overgrown with brambles in summer).

After the tree stumps, turn left down the hill to Petersham swings, past the cherry trees with horizontal rings on the bark. Don't go to the end of the path, but make your way down the hill.

19. Group of London Plane Trees. (These are on your left, after the fallen oak tree). The seeds of this tree grow in tight balls. The bark, in mottled shades of green and cream, flakes off in round patches. This peeling bark is a very useful feature for this tree which is often planted in city streets and squares. It helps the tree get rid of the dust and dirt it collects from the atmosphere.

20. The Russell School stood just inside Petersham Gate for almost a hundred years, until it was bombed in 1943. It was rebuilt on the Petersham Road. In the summer, lessons took place under the cedar trees. The school was founded by Lady Russell, wife of Lord John Russell, mentioned at item 10.

There is a children's playground here now and toilets, but no refreshments.

Turn left and walk along the shared cycle/pedestrian path.

21. All Saints, Petersham. This Romanesque church was built in 1908. It is now a grade 2 listed building which has been converted into a single dwelling.

In summer, look for wild flowers and butterflies amongst the grasses. Notice too, how many different species of grass there are.

22. Mistletoe. On the right of the shared path is a fallen lime tree with branches growing up out of its side. The mistletoe is growing high up, in one of the trees to the right. It is only visible when the tree is bare. Mistletoe is a parasite feeding on the tree on which it grows. There are many ancient myths and legends about this plant.

There is an extensive rabbit warren around this tree.

23. Cedar Trees, on the left of the shared path. Many of these trees were planted in Petersham Park, the landscaped garden belonging to Petersham Lodge, a building now lost. Some of the cedars are young (planted in the 1960s), and more are still being planted. The aim is to make this area different from the rest of the Park.

You can see that this area is more like a landscaped garden than a hunting park. Look underneath the cedars to see all the wonderful cones and catkins. When ripe, the cones separate out into flakes and each flake holds a seed.

24. Rabbit Warren underneath the cedars. This area is alive with rabbits in the summer, especially in the early evening. Every year each female rabbit (doe) produces around 20 babies (kittens).

Leave the shared path at the second bench, just where the perimeter wall ends and is replaced by railings. Take the left fork up the hill to Pembroke Lodge. (You could walk back through the gardens of Pembroke Lodge, via the gate beside the pine trees. Dogs are not allowed in the gardens or café, but you can also get refreshments at the kiosk in the car park and sit on benches outside). If you do not go through the gardens at the top of the hill, keep the railings on your left and go up the steps through the fence barrier. Turn left at the top to return to the car park.

Family Trail Number Three

Three Gates and a Dark Hill Walk

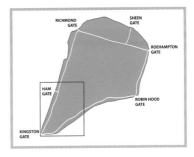

An easy walk to follow because it goes along beside the Park's perimeter wall for much of the way! Follow the path beside the wall beneath ancient oak trees to Kingston Gate. Pick your way past the adventure playground for small children, across streams and bridges and walk up the wooded hill (Dark Hill) to Ladderstile Gate. Then go across the open grass, past beech and birch trees, looking for the cork oak tree and the site of the 1948 Olympic village. Walk up a gentle hill onto the ridge-way for magnificent views and the chance of a beautiful sunset. Walk home down the slope, passing a small pond on the way.

Distance: approximately 2 miles / 3 km.
Time: 1 to 2 hours (depending on pace).

Route: From Ham Gate along beside the perimeter wall to Kingston Gate. Up Dark Hill to Ladderstile Gate and across the road towards Dann's Pond. Then across to Thatched House Lodge and down to Ham Gate.

Park outside Ham Gate and walk through the Gate.

1. Ham Gate Pond and Lodge. The pond appears on a map dated 1754 and is one of the oldest in the Park. The lodge, across the road to your right, was built in 1742. Ham Gate was one of the original gates into the park, after the enclosure in 1637. A ladderstile (step ladder over the wall) was put here in 1758, to allow pedestrians into the Park, when the gates were locked. It was here for more than a hundred years. Did you notice the letterbox built into the wall?

2. Judas Tree. This is just inside the gate on your left, before the toilets, next to the wall. It is a small tree which has simple round leaves and pretty pink pea-like flowers in late April. In winter there are pods around the seeds. There is an ancient myth that Judas Iscariot hanged himself from this type of tree. This might have arisen because the French name for it is 'Arbre de Judée', which means tree of Judea, referring to the region where this tree is common. The flowers of this tree spring open when an insect lands on them. This makes sure that pollen is transferred to other trees when the insect moves on.

Cross the road to your right and walk beside the wall toward Kingston Gate. After item 5, fork left off the busy shared cycle path onto the parallel track.

3. Pile of logs and branches. Wood is left to decay like this, in order to create a habitat for beetles, insects and fungi. These insects, in turn, are eaten by birds, as part of the complex food web.

4. King Alfred's Cake Fungus. A little further on, just past the end of the garden enclosed by a fence, there is a fallen trunk on the right of the path. The fungus is on the far side of the trunk. This is a common name for these little black/brown balls which grow on dead tree trunks.

According to a popular legend, in 877 King Alfred asked a woman for shelter whilst hiding from the Vikings. Not knowing he was the king, she asked him to watch over her cakes baking in an oven while she fetched her husband. The king was preoccupied with matters of state and let the cakes burn!

5. Drainage Ditches. All around the path are channels which have been dug out to drain away excess water. These create a different type of habitat, suitable for the wildlife which thrives in shallow, stagnant water and boggy areas. Dead wood lying in water is a special type of habitat which suits some very rare invertebrates (animals without backbones).

6. Boundary Wall. King Charles 1 built a 2m high wall to enclose the Park but did allow the common people in, for the purpose of access from one village to another, or to collect firewood. (Then there were six gates in the wall. Now there are eleven.) The public were kept out more and more as time went by and were almost totally banned in the 1750s. John Lewis, a local brewer, won public access in 1758. In 2008 the Friends of Richmond Park put up a memorial plaque to John Lewis at Sheen Gate. The public were finally given access 24 hours a day in 1894. The original wall, completed in 1637, was poorly built, and over the centuries has mostly been replaced.

Immediately before Kingston Gate you come to the enclosed Kingston Gate Garden. This is a pretty, planted garden popular with young children. Cross the road here, walk behind the children's adventure playground and go over the wooden bridge. After a few metres, you need to leave the shared path before the second wooden bridge. Look for a little track leading off into the trees straight ahead of you. Cross the little stream and step over the fallen tree. Cross two more streams and continue up the hill. As you cross another stream, look up to your right to spot the next two items.

7. 'Eyes' in the Trees. Some tree trunks look as if they have eyes watching you. These form when a branch breaks off and the trunk repairs itself. This one is on a beech tree. Beech bark is particularly thin, sometimes just 1 cm deep. It supports very few species of insect, unlike the deep, fissured bark of the ancient oak trees which attracts a multitude of creatures. In autumn mammals and birds feed on the beech nuts.

8. Tree with Black Sap. The black streak you can see has been caused by sap running out of the tree. The tree has been pruned at the top into a crown shape. Trees are pruned like this to create a suitable environment for species of insect and fungi, which help break down the dead wood. It is important to have ancient, middle-aged and young trees in an area, to maintain a range and variety of habitats. The middle-aged trees will become the ancient ones of the future.

Just before the top of the hill, cross the shared cycle path. (Watch out for the cyclists as this can be a busy junction). Walk beside the horse track, keeping an eye out for horses, all the way to Ladderstile Gate.

9. Animal Foot Prints. Look in the horse track for prints left by dogs, deer, foxes and horses. The print in the picture is one made by a dog in the snow. A fox print is different to a dog's in that all pads are the same size. In a dog the back pad is bigger. What prints can you see?

10. Young Beech Trees. The trees are protected by wooden panels (called crates) to stop the deer from scraping the bark and nibbling the branches. Beech trees have simple oval shaped leaves, with smooth edges and 10 - 12 pairs of veins on each leaf. Hornbeam leaves, which look quite similar, have 15 pairs of veins and are jagged, or toothed, around the edge.

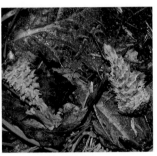

11. Pine cones around the log pile. Can you see any cones which have been eaten by squirrels? They nibble all around the cone, leaving a central stalk. This collection of evergreen pine trees attracts a range of insects and birds different from those which visit the deciduous woodland. (Deciduous trees lose their leaves in autumn).

12. Woodland birds. More than a hundred different species of bird are recorded in the Park annually. Common birds which you are likely to see are jackdaws, parakeets, crows, magpies and jays (pictured here). Smaller species you may first hear and then be able to locate by their calls, are blue tits, great tits and robins. Some birds migrate to Britain to breed during our summer: blackcaps, chiffchaffs, willow warblers and common whitethroats. Others visit to winter here, such as flocks of redwing, fieldfare, siskin and redpoll. You could take photos of the birds you see and look them up when you get home.

13. Ladderstile Gate Lodge. This is one of the six original gates into the Park. There used to be a ladderstile over the wall here in the early 18th century and from 1758 to 1884. The lodge was built in the 1780s.

Turn left on the first tarmac road at Ladderstile Lodge, with oak trees on your left and horse chestnuts (conker trees) on your right. Cross the main road and continue walking in the same direction. You will have three small beech trees on your right and three on your left, each individually protected by a fence. Walk straight ahead for about 40 metres, bearing slightly right towards the narrow path which leads you down into the wood, in the hollow. It may be boggy underfoot.

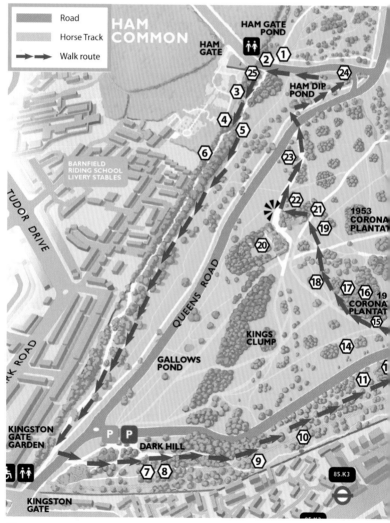

14. Deer. The open grassland here is a favourite spot for deer. There are two types of deer in the Park; the larger red deer and the smaller, spotted fallow. In Britain there are six species of deer. The others are roe, sika, muntjac and Chinese water deer. Always observe deer from a distance of at least 50 metres, and remember to keep dogs on leads whenever you are near them.

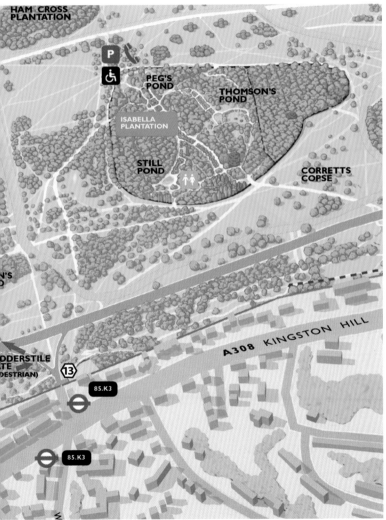

15. Beech Trees. The roots are exposed on several of these trees. Some create little pools of water and others contain rabbit holes. The leaves grow alternately along the twigs and create a very dense shade, so very little grows underneath beech trees.

Once in the hollow, turn left towards the fallen tree trunk, pictured below.

16. Cork Oak. There are only a few cork oak trees in the Park. One living cork oak stands next to this fallen stump. It is an evergreen tree which, like all oaks, produces acorns. It originates from the Mediterranean. There the bark is often stripped off every eight to ten years and used to make corks for wine bottles. The bark grows back again a few years later.

17. Woodpecker Practice Tree! This is immediately left of the cork oak. Woodpeckers drum on trees, especially in the spring, to mark out their territory. They make more noise by drumming on hollow wood. They usually dig out nest holes in soft, rotten wood because it is easier making a new hole each year. Abandoned holes are taken over by other birds like parakeets.

The woodpecker's head is adapted to cope with all the hammering. It has shock-absorbing cartilage between its beak and skull - an evolutionary development to protect its brain.

Carry straight on across the muddy hollow to the white trunks of the silver birch trees. When you come to a path, look for the concrete steps to your left.

18. Kingston Gate Camp. The grassy area above the steps was an army camp in 1938 for the East Surrey Regiment. Later it was used as a military convalescent home, and by the Women's Royal Army Corps (WRAC). It became the Olympic Village in 1948 when Britain last hosted the Games - rather different from the Olympic Village for 2012 athletes! In 1956 it was a hostel for service families evacuated from the Suez Canal Zone. These concrete steps are all that remain.

Go up the steps and turn right immediately. Continue on the path past the birch trees on your left. Fork right and head for the circular plantation of beech trees, enclosed by a fence. This is Coronation Plantation, planted to commemorate the coronation of Queen Elizabeth II in 1953. Just before you reach the plantation, follow the path to the left and head for the small group of oak trees. NB. There are actually two Coronation Plantations very close to each other. The other one commemorates the coronation of Edward VII in 1902.

19. Two Oak Trees from one base! On your right, it looks as if there are four large oak trees, but really two are growing from the same roots. If you were to estimate the age of this oak by measuring it in hugs, what would you do? It is on the Royal Parks tree database and the nation's Tree Register as an ancient tree, but as one tree or two?
Find out more at www.treeregister.org

Carry on, crossing over a footpath, keeping the cottage garden surrounded by a fence on your left.

20. Thatched House Lodge. In the 1670s this was originally a small building for the Park's deer keepers. It is Princess Alexandra's private residence and is not open to the public.

21. Upturned Tree. The textures and colours inside the roots are wonderful. This tree was probably uprooted in a storm - possibly the Great Storm of 1987 when Richmond Park and Kew Gardens lost thousands of trees. Like many others in the Park, this one has been left to decay.

Keeping the fence to your left, head for the benches with views over Kingston.

22. Bench and Owls. This is the perfect place to watch the sunset and listen to the owls. Owls are common in the Park with possibly 15 pairs of tawny owl and 30 pairs of little owl.

Tawny owls (upper picture) are mottled dark brown and white, with a pattern which camouflages well with oak tree bark. They hunt at night and generally occupy the woods.

Little owls (lower picture) are smaller and sometimes seen in the day. They have flecked brown and white feathers, yellow eyes and white eyebrows! They are generally found at woodland edges. Little owls feed mainly on beetles and earth worms.

Owls gobble their prey whole then spit out the bones and fur later, in the form of sausage-shaped pellets. If you are very lucky, you might find one under an owl's perch or roosting post.

Turn right by the benches and walk down the hill along the concrete road, to the main road.

23. Bark of a False Acacia. This is on your left on the way down the road. The lattice pattern on the bark looks as if it is made out of twisted ropes. It is a similar pattern to the sweet chestnut, but less regular. The tree is an introduced species, quite common around the Park. Look for the distinctive spines on the young branches. There might be fungus growing inside the trunk hole. Look at the beautiful markings around the hole which are rather like the arch of a church window.

Cross the main road and turn right along the tarmac footpath which runs beside the road. Stay on this path down the hill. Follow the grassy track off to your left, just before the railings appear next to the road. You will be able to see Ham Dip Pond on your left. This track will lead you back to Ham Gate, where the walk began.

24. Ham Dip Pond. This is next to the road. This little pond was dug out in 1861, along with eight other ponds in the Park. This was part of a programme to deal with the boggy areas and provide better drinking facilities for the deer.

25. Dr. Who's Tardis! Did you notice this on the way in? It's an old police box. A police force was set up in the Park in 1854 after a lady visiting the Prime Minister, Lord Russell, had her watch and jewellery stolen at pistol point. There is a police station at Holly Lodge.

Family Trail Number Four

See -Through Tree Walk

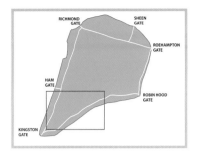

This walk leads you through ancient woodland into the beautiful Isabella Plantation. Set off across open grassland and go up the wooded hill to the 'See-through Tree'. Passing a row of birch trees, explore the medieval wood, rich in wildlife and wonderful trees. At the bottom of the hill, enter the magical world of the Isabella Plantation. Enjoy the duck pond, the stepping stones and the pretty streams. Come home across the open grassland, looking out for butterflies or fungi, depending on the season.

Distance: approximately 2.5 miles / 4 km. Time: 1 to 2 hours (depending on pace).

Route: From Kingston Gate to Thatched House Lodge. Past Dann's Pond, into the Isabella Plantation and back to Kingston Gate.

With Kingston Gate and the car park behind you, cross the road at the car park exit. Walk straight ahead, parallel to the main road leading to Ham Gate, heading for a pond which is hidden from view, down in the dip.

1. Ant Hills. The bumps in the grass are made by ants not moles. There are no longer any moles in the Park. Each ant hill has been made by a single colony of yellow meadow ants, which could number up to 14,000. Some mounds are decades or even centuries old and each contains a network of tunnels which are kept at an even temperature by the mass of soil above. Please do not tread on or damage them in any way.

The green woodpecker pecks into these mounds to feed on the ants. Their feathers are camouflaged to blend with the grassland. Grasshoppers lay their eggs on the ant hills and butterflies (like the peacock, pictured here) and reptiles use them to bask in the sun.

2. Gallows Pond. This pond is named after the gallows which were just outside Kingston Gate. Jerry Abershaw, a well-known highwayman, was hanged there in 1795. Deer come to drink here in the early morning. It is full of frogspawn in the spring. In summer the emperor dragonflies and small damselflies dart around. You might even see a grass snake swimming here.

3. Sugar Maples, above Gallows Pond. A hundred of these trees were planted here in 1969 as a gift from the Government of Ontario, to mark the centenary of Ontario's representation in London. They commemorate the Canadian troops stationed in the Park during World War II. These trees turn a spectacular shade of red in the autumn.

From the pond, continue straight ahead up the hill, on the footpath behind the bench.

4. Bark scraped by deer antlers. This is on your right just before the blasted oak (that is, one that has been damaged by an explosive force, such as lightning). Can you see scratches at the base of some beech trees? In autumn male deer scrape the trees with their antlers to mark their territory.

5. Log Pile. The 'sawn-through' tree stumps, to your left, have patterns of concentric rings. These are annual rings. The trunk grows a new one every year. By counting the rings you can estimate a tree's age.

6. Hollow Tree, near the top of the hill. Several of the ancient oak trees in the Park are hollow but still alive. The thick centre of the tree, the heartwood, is the oldest part. It is made up of dead water-carrying tubes. The important, living part is the cambium layer, just inside the bark. As this is a deer park, the majority of trees produce seeds which are eaten by the deer: oak, horse chestnut, sweet chestnut and beech.

7. 'See-Through Tree'. A wonderful old oak tree, which is still alive despite its traumatic past. What do you think may have happened to it? Look up to see the woodpecker hole on the left bough. Parakeets may nest in there now.

At the hill top cross the tarmac drive and walk straight ahead on the track beside the silver birches. Keep the small wooden enclosure on your right.

8. Silver Birch Trees. Notice the black and white bark. Bark is like the tree's skin, which protects its insides from damage. It has natural breathing holes, to let air in. These look like blisters or very thin strips. Some of these birch trees have been coppiced. This is an ancient method of woodland management where the trunk is cut back almost to the ground to encourage new shoots.

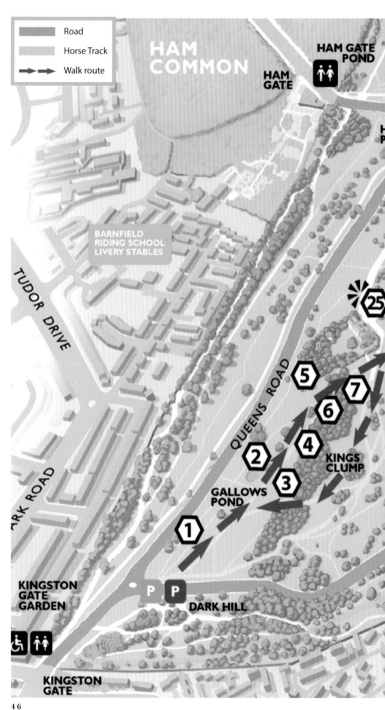

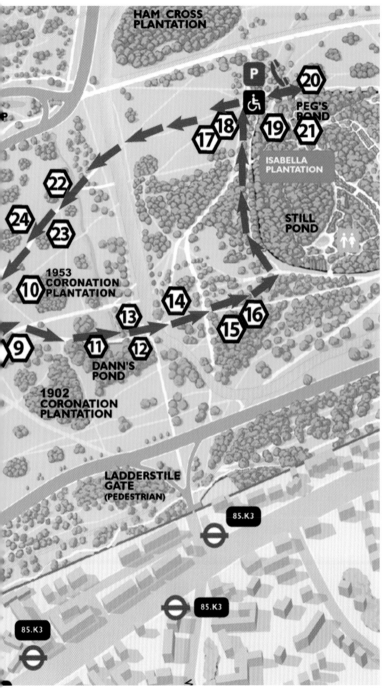

9. Traces of a tennis court. If you look carefully on the ground, on either side of the small wooden enclosure, you may find the bases of the metal posts which were used for a tennis court. The metal base on the further side of the enclosure, (as you walk by) is actually inscribed with the words 'Championship Tennis'.

The tennis court dates back to Kingston Gate Camp, which was established in 1938 for the East Surrey Regiment. During the Second World War the Park would have looked very different. Large areas were ploughed up for crops. Pen Ponds were drained and camouflaged to prevent them being used as a landmark by enemy planes. After the war, there was an athletics village on this site, for the 1948 Olympic Games, held in London.

10. Coronation Plantation. Over to your left across the open ground, is a circle of beech trees, surrounded by railings. These were planted in 1953 to celebrate Queen Elizabeth II's coronation. The trees on your right were planted in 1902, to celebrate the coronation of Edward VII, the Queen's great-grandfather. It may seem odd that there are two 'Coronation Plantations' planted so close to each other.

When you have Coronation Plantation (surrounded by railings) on your left, take the right fork in front of the solitary oak tree. Almost immediately afterwards, at the junction of four paths, turn left heading down into the dip. The woodland around Dann's Pond, enclosed by railings, will soon be on your right.

11. Dann's Pond. Look through the railings to your right. This pond is often covered with algae in the summer. It has been here since at least 1754. It is fenced off, to create a safe environment for wildlife. In spring you can see mandarin ducks and coots (pictured next page).

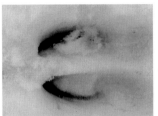

The enclosure contains dense scrub (rare in the Park) which is useful cover for birds such as blackcap, chiffchaff and song thrush to breed in. The undisturbed wetland habitat is good for amphibians such as frogs, toads and newts.

12. Animal Tracks. Are there any prints on the path? You can tell how fast an animal was moving, from the distance between each set of tracks. If they are far apart and in pairs, it was running. Deer tracks are known as 'slots'. Look for prints in the shape of two half ovals (pictured here).

13. Worm Casts. Are there little squiggly heaps of earth on the muddy path? Worms eat earth as well as dead leaves. The waste passes through their body and comes out in these small piles.

Cross the horse track into the wood and stay on the path straight ahead, keeping the hollow tree, pictured below, on your left.

14. Hollow Tree in High Wood. The hollow inside the tree was probably created when a large branch broke away from the trunk, leaving the dead heartwood at the centre of the trunk exposed. This has rotted away over the years. These hollow trees provide good nesting sites for breeding birds, bats and insects. High Wood is one of the oldest woods in the Park, dating back to medieval times. Charles I enclosed the Park for hunting in the 1630s. Large parts of the area were already a royal hunting ground. The other areas which were privately owned were bought by Charles I.

When a large oak tree enclosed by a fence blocks your path, look for item 15 to your right. Walk around the oak, keeping it on your left. This will take you onto a path which leads straight ahead.

15. Christmas Trees! The evergreen cedar looks like a very tall Christmas tree all year round. Look at the tightly packed cones on the ground beneath the tree. There are two larch trees to the right of the cedar. The larch is a deciduous conifer. This means it loses its leaves in the autumn. It has much smaller cones than the cedar, with several on each branch. The female cones are soft and bright red in the spring. They turn brown later in the year.

16. 'Owl' Tree. This is the next big tree on your right, after the junction. You need to look up! Parts of the trunk and branches of this oak tree look like an owl. It seems to have big round eyes and a beak. Owls are common and widespread in the Park, with possibly 15 pairs of tawny owl and 30 pairs of little owl. The tawny generally occupies woods and the little owl is found at woodland edges. Tawny owls have a varied diet of small mammals (voles, mice and shrews), frogs, earthworms, beetles and smaller birds. Little owls eat mainly earthworms and beetles and some small mammals.

Just before you reach the second fence across the path, around the ancient oak, turn sharp left and walk up to the fence enclosing the Isabella Plantation, which is full of dark green rhododendron bushes. Turn left and walk down the hill, keeping the fence on your right, until you reach the second gate into the Isabella Plantation, at the disabled car park. You can see Peg's Pond through the gate.

17. Deer. There is a good chance of seeing deer on the open grassland here. There are two types of deer in the Park, the large red deer and the smaller, speckled fallow deer. Male red deer are called stags and females, hinds. The young are calves. Male fallow deer are called bucks and the females, does. Their young are fawns. Only the male deer grow antlers. They cast (drop) their antlers each spring and new ones grow back immediately, protected by a soft covering known as 'velvet'. When the antlers are fully grown, their blood supply is cut off and the deer clean away the velvet, in time for the autumn rut (breeding season).

18. Beech Trees just by the gate. On the ground you may see nuts and shells called beech mast. Beech leaves grow alternately along the twigs, so that they receive maximum sunlight. The trees cast such dense shade that very little grows beneath them. Beech leaves often cling to the branches through the winter.

19. Isabella Plantation. This was planted in 1831 by Lord Sidmouth. The name is more than 200 years old, but its origin is unclear. Water is pumped up from Pen Ponds, to add to the flow through the plantation. The Isabella Plantation is particularly beautiful in April and May, when the camellias, azaleas and rhododendrons are in bloom. It is a wonderful place to visit all year round, particularly by the ponds and streams. The variety of trees and plants attract various species of birds and insect.

20. Peg's Pond. All kinds of ducks live here. There are wild birds such as mallards, brightly coloured mandarins (pictured here) and diving tufted ducks. Also birds of captive origin such as the shoveler, with wide flat beaks; large white shelduck, with black heads and red beaks; and the elegant grey and brown pintail.

Walk around the pond to your right, to the Heather Garden, crossing over a small, wooden bridge. Then navigation gets a bit trickier! Turn right up the path. Then second left, followed by first right to the stepping stones and little stream. This is the Bog Garden.

21. Heather and Bog Gardens. There is such a variety of textures and colours in the planting here, it is stunning all year round. In summer the Bog Garden is particularly dramatic with huge gunnera plants hanging over the stream and dragonflies darting above the water. Children love to play on the stepping stones.

Make your way back to the gate where you came in, and leave the Isabella. With your back to the gate, go to the bench. Take the third path from the left, which leads across grassland towards a line of trees in the dip. Cross the horse track and head for the bridge to get across the stream, as it can be very boggy in the dip. Follow the footpath back up the hill to Thatched House Lodge.

22. Brick bridge across the stream. Some birds, such as waders, are especially adapted to feed in boggy areas such as this. Winter visitors like woodcock and snipe might come here to search for food with their long, pointed beaks. They are deeply camouflaged, so you would be incredibly lucky to see one!

23. Butterflies. In summer look out for different butterflies and day-flying moths feeding on the grasses. Pictured is a gatekeeper, a common wayside butterfly. You might see skippers too, which are smaller orange-brown butterflies with the forewing angled up. The name derives from their swift, bouncing flight pattern. They have quite wide, furry bodies. There are three species of skipper in the Park- small, large (lower picture) and Essex.

24. Fungi. In autumn you may see different species of fungi underneath the beech trees to the right of the footpath. Fly agaric, pictured here, is a poisonous fungus, so **do not touch it.** It usually grows under birch trees but sometimes grows here.

When you have the beech trees on your right, keep straight ahead. Do not fork left to the large, circular plantation. Look out for deer at the top of the ridge, silhouetted against the skyline. The footpath bears left to Thatched House Lodge.

25. Thatched House Lodge. The original lodge dates from 1673. Sir Robert Walpole, Britain's first Prime Minister, improved it and added a thatched summer house in 1727. By 1771 the entire building was known as Thatched House Lodge.

At Thatched House Lodge join the tarmac drive and continue on the path straight ahead, walking on the crest of the hill above the wood. When you reach the second bench, you will be at Kings Clump, a small enclosure of pine trees. From here head down the hill to the car park.

Family Trail Number Five

Distant Views Walk

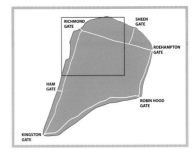

The perfect walk for a clear day as the views can be marvellous. Start with a view through the trees to St Paul's Cathedral and then a view downhill to Ham House and the River Thames. Walking just inside the perimeter wall, visit the ducks on Bishop's Pond. Go through a wood and cross open grassland, passing more ponds and gorse enclosures, an area rich in wildlife. See if the shire horses are in their paddock, then climb the hill to a plantation of sweet chestnut trees. Deer often rest here and you might hear a woodpecker. On the way home, if the skies are clear, look back for some wonderful views of the London skyline.

Distance: approximately 3 miles / 4.5 km.
Time: 1.5 to 2.5 hours (depending on pace).
This is the longest walk, but can be cut down.

Route: From Pembroke Lodge towards Richmond Gate, past Bishop's Pond into Conduit Wood. Around the edge of Holly Lodge, through Barn Wood, past Barn Wood Pond and up through Saw Pit Plantation, around the outside of Sidmouth Wood and back to Pembroke Lodge.

Start in front of the Information/Visitor Centre, which is at the back of Pembroke Lodge car park. With Pembroke Lodge behind you, turn left and walk along beside the railings toward Richmond Gate. When the path divides, stay on the path to your left, next to the railings, and furthest away from the road.

1. View to St Paul's Cathedral. As you go along the path, look for the stone circle on the ground. When you reach this marker, look to your right and on a clear day you will have an uninterrupted view to St Paul's Cathedral, ten miles away.

55

The trees in Sidmouth Wood on the opposite side of the road are cut back to maintain this view, which has existed for 300 years. Now look for item 2, immediately to your left.

2. King Henry's Mound. This is another viewpoint through to St Paul's, accessible from inside Pembroke Lodge gardens. There is a telescope on this little hill. Note that only guide dogs are allowed in these gardens. According to an old tale, Henry VIII stood here on May 19th 1536. He was waiting for a rocket signal that his wife Anne Boleyn had been executed at The Tower and he could marry Jane Seymour. The story appears not to be true as there is evidence Henry hunted in Wiltshire that day.

3. S - Shaped Wrought Iron Bench, called 'The Poet's Seat'. Just outside Pembroke Lodge gardens there is an ironwork bench with views down to the Thames, Petersham Meadows and Ham House (pictured here). The inscription on the bench, which is now hard to read, consists of lines from a poem called 'The Seasons', written by James Thomson, the 18th century Richmond poet. The seat was installed in 1994 in memory of Ramon Osner, a founder of the Kingston Riding Centre and a passionate lover of the Park.

4. Dead Tree Monolith. You may see stump puffball fungus at the base of this dead tree and in the log pile. Look for small grey/pale brown balls about 2cm wide, growing out of the dead wood. Some balls have a hole in the top, through which thousands of spores have exploded. Spores are a very simple type of seed, which are fine as dust. Mind the stinging nettles.

5. Lime Tree. This is a remnant of a much older tree. Look at the girth of the remaining trunk at ground level. This tree is listed as a veteran - that is, one which, because of age, size or condition, is considered to be of exceptional value. All the veteran trees in the Park are listed. This one is still alive although almost all the trunk has broken away. Lime tree leaves are asymmetrical, and in summer are often covered in tiny insects.

Cross the road just inside Richmond Gate and walk, with the perimeter wall on your left, along the gravel path to Bishop's Pond.

6. Beetle Holes inside the Sycamore trunk. This is just by the green, wildlife information sign. The tiny holes are evidence that beetles have been here. Beetles which feed on dead or decaying wood are called saproxylic beetles. They release nutrients in the wood for the benefit of the trees and plants. Some of these (eg some species of click beetle) are extremely rare and exist only in a few sites in the UK.

7. 'Hippopotamus' Tree Stump and Butterflies. Do you think this stump, on your left, looks like a hippopotamus standing on its back legs? The brambles and nettles are important for butterflies. The comma and red admiral lay their eggs on nettle plants and the caterpillars of the peacock and red admiral feed on nettles. The red admiral is a migrating butterfly which overwinters in Spain. The others hibernate in the Park.

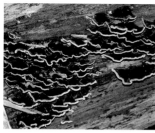

8. Fungi on Dead Wood. This is next to item 7. These dead tree stumps are the perfect place for fungi to grow and tiny insects to live. Like the beetles, some species of fungi help to decompose the dead wood. The brambles look untidy but they provide good cover and food for birds. The fungus in the photo is turkeytail. You may see other fungi like jelly ear and coral-spot.

9. Bishop's Pond. This first appears on a map dated 1861. There are often mallards and mandarin ducks here and the occasional heron (pictured). The alder trees next to the pond, with their pretty cones and catkins, provide food for small birds such as goldfinch and, in winter, siskin and redpoll. Bishop's Gate used to be known as the 'Cattle Gate'. In the nineteenth century, there were two wooden gates here which let cattle into the Park to graze. It was opened for public access in 1896, after a successful petition from local residents. Please respect the 'no dogs in the pond' signs, where present, as dogs do cause damage to the wildlife in the ponds.

Ignore the left fork down to Cambrian Gate, after you have passed Bishop's Pond and the small pond on your left.

10. Cambrian Gate and the South African Military Hospital. In the First World War, the area between Bishop's Pond and Conduit Wood was used for a hospital. Cambrian Gate (off to your left) was opened to allow access. The hospital buildings were rows of wooden huts on brick stands. They were demolished in

1925. Local cemeteries contain the graves of South Africans who died here from their wounds. A new pond has been dug next to Cambrian Gate, to retain water in the Park to combat the drier weather forecast because of climate change. The long, red brick building outside the Park, over to the right, has been built on the site of the Richmond Parish Workhouse.

Just after Cambrian Gate, turn right at the junction of two paths by the low marker with a sign for 'No Horses'. Walk straight ahead, crossing over the horse track. Take the second grassy track to your right, leading into Conduit Wood. You will have several small stake-fenced enclosures on your left.

11. Three Trunked Beech Tree! As you go into Conduit Wood, planted in 1829, look for this tree on your right. Long ago it was coppiced, or cut down at the base, to encourage new trunks to grow. This is a traditional method which increased the production of timber. Notice all the water holes at the base of the tree. See how thin and smooth the bark is, compared to that of an oak tree.

Turn off the track to your right, to find White Conduit (item 12).

12. White Conduit. This low, domed building, which covers a spring, is known by children as 'the air raid shelter'. The conduit is probably the oldest surviving structure in the Park, pre-dating the Park's enclosure in the seventeenth century. It was dug in about 1500 to supply water to the Palace of Shene on Richmond Green, and some of the original Tudor brick remains. It was at this time that King Henry VII decided that the settlement called Shene was to be known as Richmond. He had been the Earl of Richmond - the town in Yorkshire. King Henry VIII lived in this Palace and Queen Elizabeth I died there.

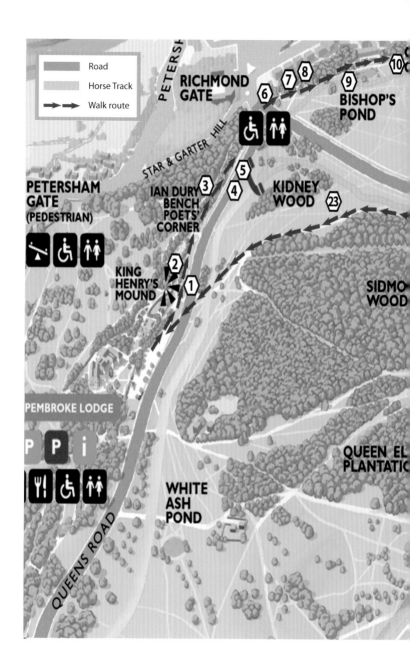

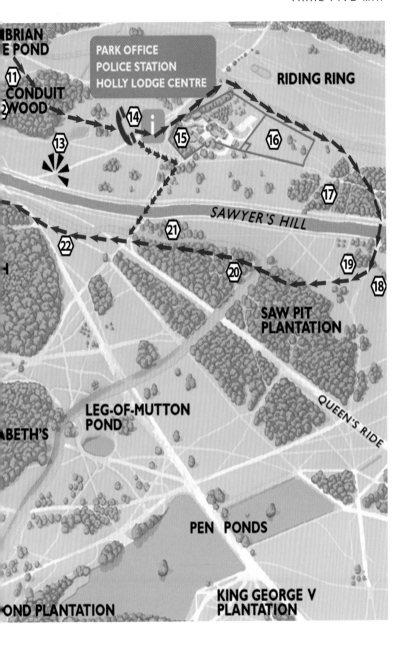

BRIAN
E POND

11

CONDUIT
WOOD

PARK OFFICE
POLICE STATION
HOLLY LODGE CENTRE

RIDING RING

14

i

15

16

13

17

SAWYER'S HILL

21

22

19

20

18

SAW PIT
PLANTATION

QUEEN'S RIDE

LEG-OF-MUTTON
POND

BETH'S

PEN PONDS

KING GEORGE V
PLANTATION

OND PLANTATION

After item 12 walk downhill along the path to the small bridge over the Conduit stream. There is a small pond to your left. Stay on this path and go slightly uphill out of the wood to a bigger pond.

13. Conduit Pond. Another pond, popular with dogs! In summer, emperor dragonflies dart around, defending their territory. Their wingspan is about 10cm. You might also see smaller, common blue damselflies or broad bodied chasers. Notice the thorn and gorse enclosures as you move away from the pond. These are here for the wildlife and birds which are attracted to them, for example the whitethroat.

Turn sharp left away from the pond to the ancient oak tree. Continue past the large gorse enclosure then turn right and walk beside the row of ancient oaks. Continue until you reach the fence around the Holly Lodge complex of buildings.

14. Line of Ancient Oaks. These oaks are medieval, 600 to 700 years old. They were probably once in a hedgerow, marking out the boundary of fields belonging to Hill Farm which before 1637 stretched from here to where the wall is now.

15. Holly Lodge. (On this walk, you will see the outbuildings at the back of Holly Lodge and not Holly Lodge itself.) This used to be called Bog Lodge! This houses the Royal Parks' office and workshops; the Metropolitan Police station; stables and the Holly Lodge Centre charity, providing education for those with special needs. The Park office is open for information, 09.00 - 16.00, Monday to Friday. The original building at the front dates back to the 1730s. It was the head keeper's lodge.

At the fence, turn left and walk along beside the grounds of Holly Lodge. Follow the fence round to your right. Look out for skylarks singing above the open grassland, known as The Bog, on your left. (Note: As this is a long walk, you might wish to head back at this stage. If you do, bear right before you reach the Holly Lodge complex and head for the access road. Follow it back to the main road. Pick up the walk between items 21 and 22.)

16. Shire Horse Paddock. There are two shire horses living here, an old one and a young one. Horses worked in the Park for more than 300 years until 1954. They were brought back in 1993. They work about twenty hours a week on jobs like cutting the grass verges, rolling the bracken, chain harrowing and general carting duties. In summer, they represent the Royal Parks at local shows and fairs, where they wear a show harness and their manes and tails are plaited with colourful ribbons. Look out for different species of bird in the paddock, attracted by a range of insects in the horse manure and the grazed grass. With binoculars, you might spot a little owl, and there are almost always rabbits to be seen here.

Walk along beside the paddock with the fence on your right. Where the fence meets the wood, go into the wood and follow the middle track downhill to the road.

17. Barn Wood. This is a medieval wood, one of the oldest in the Park. The sunken track, which you can walk down, is Deane's Lane and in medieval times was the main road from Mortlake to Ham. To the right, partly in the woods and partly in the open ground, you may be able to see the furrows and ridges that are the marks of ploughing in medieval times. This is best seen close to the ground. Look out for woodland birds: jackdaws, magpies, parakeets and robins. Can you see any nest holes in the trees?

Cross the road at the bottom of the wood. Look to your left for a small pond surrounded by fallen trees. Follow the track up the hill, bearing right towards the large wood, Saw Pit Plantation.

18. Deer. Deer are often to be seen near Barn Wood Pond, on your left before you go up the hill, or in the bracken below the wood. The jackdaw, catching a lift on the back of this red deer hind might be looking for ticks to eat. Ticks attach themselves to the deer and feed on their blood. They can feed on humans too, so keep your legs covered! Check your dog too, after a walk in the Park.

19. Butterflies. In the summer, look out for butterflies on the bracken: red admiral, peacock, purple hairstreak and tiny skippers. In the woods you may see speckled wood (pictured here) and in the grasses, meadow brown and small heath.

Turn right onto a small muddy track as soon as you get into the wood. The path then joins the horse track. Continue straight on, beside the horse track.

20. Hoof Prints in the Mud. Have the shire horses been along this track? Their prints are enormous. Can you see the horses in their paddock, over to your right?

21. Kestrels. The tall trees to the right of the track provide a good vantage point over the bracken and open grassland. They are an ideal spot for kestrels – birds of prey which can hover in a fixed position in the sky, scanning for food. The rough, tussocky grass is the perfect home for voles and shrews, which form a major part of a kestrel's diet.

Stay beside the horse track to the end of the wood, and beyond across the open grass to the enclosed Sidmouth Wood. Look back to your left for fine views of Queen's Ride and Pen Ponds.

22. Views of London. When you reach the bench look back to your right for wonderful views of London. Look for the new Wembley Stadium (to your left), the Shard, the London Eye, St Paul's Cathedral and the Gherkin.

Walk around the outside of Sidmouth Wood, keeping the railings on your left.

23. Acid Grassland. On the edge of Sidmouth Wood is the site of the disused reservoir which originally supplied water to Kew Gardens. When you have rounded the corner of Sidmouth Wood, you might be able to make out two low mounds which cover later reservoirs. The roofs of these disused reservoirs are actually some of the best areas of acid grassland in the Park, because the soil over them is so thin and impoverished. This type of grassland develops on acidic soils which are low in nutrients. This habitat is nationally important for a huge range of grasses, flowers (such as the harebell pictured here), fungi, invertebrates, birds and small mammals.

Richmond Park has the largest area of acid grassland in the South-East and it is one of the three reasons why it is a SSSI (Site of Special Scientific Interest), the others being its veteran trees and its saproxylic beetles.

Continue around the edge of Sidmouth Wood, keeping the railings on your left. Cross the road back to Pembroke Lodge, when you are level with the car park.

Family Trail Number Six

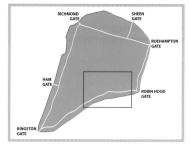

The Ponds Walk

A walk which leads you up and down hills to a number of very different ponds. Start off downhill through a wood of sweet chestnut trees and walk around Prince Charles's Spinney out onto the open grassland. Climb another steep hill overlooking Pen Ponds and go down the other side to discover a dark, mysterious pond in the middle of the wood. Come out and walk across the open grass to another pond surrounded by willow trees and bracken. Climb the hill to get home again, watching out for deer on the way.

Distance: approximately 2 miles / 3 km. **Time:** 1 to 2 hours (depending on pace).

Route: Start at Broomfield Hill car park, by the Isabella Plantation, between Kingston and Robin Hood Gates. Through Gibbet Wood, around Prince Charles's Spinney past Tercentenary Plantation. Up into Spankers Hill Wood, down to the pond, around the bottom of the wood, then across to Martin's Pond. Return to the car park around the other side of Prince Charles's Spinney.

Leave the car park at the exit closest to the refreshment van. Cross the road and walk to the end of the small fir tree enclosure. Turn right and walk along beside the enclosure towards the wood. Continue in this direction and cross a track. With the low direction post to your right, walk forward 10m, then find the path on the left downhill to a bench. When you reach the fence around Prince Charles's Spinney, turn left. Do not go into the Spinney but walk around the outside keeping the fence on your right.

1. Prince Charles's Spinney was planted in 1951, when the Prince was three. A spinney is a small wood. In the spring it is full of daffodils and bluebells. Much of the woodland is closed off to protect the wildlife. The Spinney is undergoing major thinning-out and replanting.

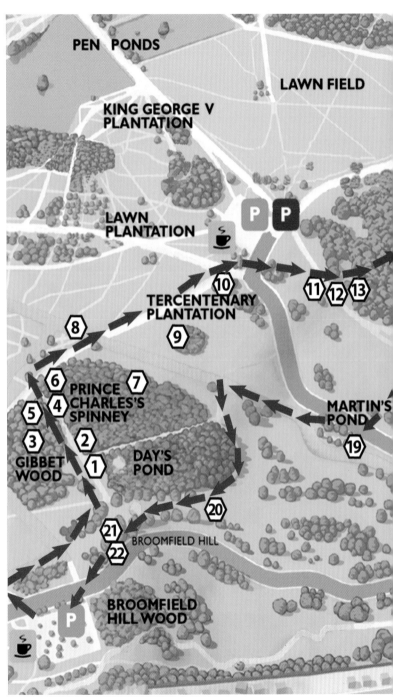

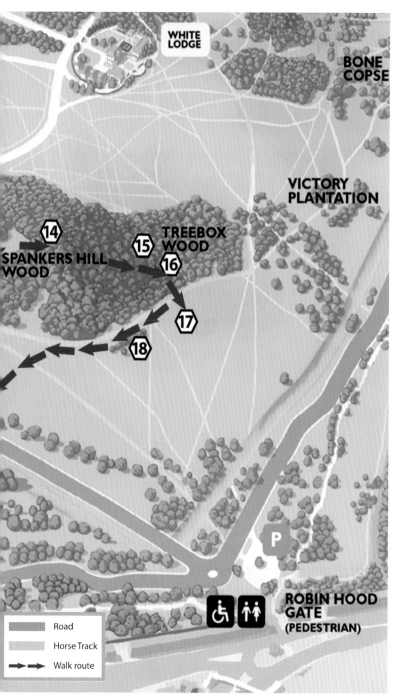

WHITE LODGE

BONE COPSE

VICTORY PLANTATION

(14)

(15) TREEBOX WOOD

(16)

SPANKERS HILL WOOD

(17)

(18)

P

ROBIN HOOD GATE (PEDESTRIAN)

Road

Horse Track

Walk route

Day's Pond is inside the Spinney, to the right. This was dug out in 2009 and is named in memory of the member of staff who created it. It will provide a wonderful new environment for the wildlife in the area. It looks beautiful with the ancient oak trees at the side.

2. Handkerchief Tree or Dove Tree. To the left of the stile is a tree which produces white bracts (modified leaves at the base of a flower) in May. These look just like handkerchiefs! It has large, oval berries in the autumn and is native to China.

3. Sweet Chestnut Trees, on your left. Look at the lattice pattern on the bark. On old sweet chestnuts the lattice appears to spiral up the trunk of the tree. The deer eat the chestnuts when they are out of their prickly cases. Chestnuts were part of the basic diet for Roman soldiers and this is why the Romans introduced the trees into Britain. They must have been planning a long occupation!

Sweet and horse chestnut trees were planted in the Park to provide food for the deer in the autumn. They are of little value to the native invertebrates (insects without backbones), perhaps because they were introduced relatively recently. A small bird called a nuthatch uses the crevices in the bark to secure a nut while it pecks at the shell to get inside. Can you see any nutshells wedged there?

4. Beetle Galleries, on a tree to your right, just outside the Spinney. These marks were left by beetle larvae as they crawled around under the bark. The dead wood is so lacking in nutrition that many species of beetle larvae take years to develop into adults.

Each species of beetle (such as the stag beetle pictured here) creates its own pattern of beetle gallery. The central tunnel, where the mother lays her eggs, is called the mother tunnel. The male helps her to dig this out. The larvae create their own tunnel, as they feed, usually at right angles to the mother tunnel. The larvae tunnels never intersect with each other. When the larvae have developed, they make a hole in the bark and emerge into the world. Daylight at last! Look up to see the rather larger holes made in the trunk by woodpeckers.

5. Slices of Tree Stump, to your left. Birds and squirrels use these flat stumps as a feeding table. Look at the shells to see who has been feeding there. Squirrels rip the nuts open but birds just peck holes into the shell.

When you meet a track coming down the hill, turn right and follow this around the enclosure.

6. Different Ages of Silver Birch Tree. Inside the Spinney on your right, you can see three silver birch trees in a row, displaying how the bark changes as the tree ages. The youngest one, in the middle, has smooth, green bark. The middle-aged tree on its right has white bark. On its left, the oldest and thickest tree has white bark with dark green / black cracks.

Leave the enclosure and continue on this broad track towards the bench and Pen Ponds car park in the distance. Two young trees, individually enclosed by fences, will be on your left.

7. New Hazel Planting, inside the Spinney to your right. The trees need the protective, green sleeves to keep away the rabbits. Hazel has been chosen because the leaves come out after the bluebells have flowered, so they can grow and bloom in full sunlight. Hazel has also been selected because it should attract more bats and different bird species. The hazelnuts will be eaten by small mammals and birds, and moth larvae will feed on the leaves.

Cross the horse track and continue to Pen Ponds car park.

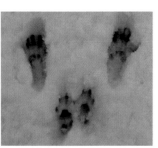

8. Animal Prints. When you cross the horse track, look for prints in the mud. You may see ones made by deer, fox, dog, horse or even birds. Animal prints are easiest to spot in the snow, or when the mud is damp. The picture shows the prints left in the snow by a squirrel.

9. Tercentenary Plantation, to your right. This was planted in 1937 to celebrate the 300th anniversary of the enclosure of the Park by Charles I. It contains oak and silver birch trees. Silver birch woods are rich in fungi.

You may see skylarks above the open grassland. Stonechats often associate with the rarer Dartford warbler in the bracken, during autumn or winter. In summer you may spot butterflies feeding on the purple thistle heads and yellow ragwort.

Follow the path to Pen Ponds Car Park.

10. Horse Chestnut (Conker) Trees, just before the road. The bark on this tree peels off in flakes, as the trunk expands. The twigs have large sticky buds in winter. Note the way some of the trees' roots have emerged above the ground.

Cross the tarmac path and, at the refreshment van and benches, cross the road on your right. Head up the hill between the large evergreen cedar tree and the tree surrounded by dead branches (item 11).

11. Largest Sycamore in the Park. The trunk of this tree is unusually flat. The roots above the ground have created pools of stagnant water, which are a special habitat, ideal for some invertebrates. Can you see the beetle holes inside the trunk?

12. Stag Beetle Loggery. (This is just beyond item 11). Logs about 3 foot long are buried deep in the earth to create a habitat for stag beetle larvae. Please do not walk on them. The larvae eat decaying wood. They take about 5 years to develop into adults.

Go to the top of the hill, bearing slightly right.

13. 'Kissing Tree', to the right. The two main branches of this sycamore tree have fused together.

Follow the path round to the left, around the rhododendron. This opens out on the other side of the wood.

14. Sweet Chestnut Trees. The lattice pattern on these trees is interrupted by great growths like footballs in a string bag.

Go down to the pond on your left.

15. Dark Pond. This was originally dug out to provide a watering hole for cattle. There are several dead logs and branches in the water. This might look unsightly but certain species of very rare invertebrates can only survive in submerged dead wood. Please keep your children and dogs out of the water to preserve this special environment. Grey wagtails can sometimes be seen here.

Turn right and go to the edge of the wood.

16. Pine Trees. These trees are protected against damage from deer and rabbits by stake fencing. Look how different the bark is from that of the silver birch and sweet chestnut. Can you see the pine tree with several woodpecker holes in the trunk and beetle holes near the base? The ground in this wood is covered in leaf litter and decaying wood. This is the perfect habitat for all kinds of invertebrates; millipedes, woodlice and beetles thrive in it. Jackdaws often forage for food here by turning over the leaves. They are the smallest member of the crow family and are one of the commonest birds in the Park. They nest in tree holes and are black with some grey on the head and neck. They are inquisitive and often seen in flocks.

Come out of the wood. Turn right and walk just below the wood, towards the small enclosures with railings.

17. Winter Feeding Manger. This is to your left, outside the wood. In hard winters the deer may not all survive just by grazing and browsing trees and bushes. Their diet has to be supplemented with hay, maize and deer pellets, which the Park wildlife officers put out for them..

18. Small Enclosures. The trees and bushes in here provide vegetation and shelter for birds and insects, away from the deer who usually eat the branches. Can you see the prickly gorse with yellow flowers?

After the enclosures, leave the path by the bench where it curves right and walk across the grass to the nearest road. Head towards the road which you can see up on the hill ahead of you, to find item 19. Cross the lower road to see Martin's Pond.

19. Martin's Pond. This appears on a map dated 1861. You might see Egyptian geese and rainbow-coloured mandarin ducks here.

Join the horse track to the right of the pond and walk alongside it, up the hill. Turn left at the bottom of Prince Charles's Spinney and follow the path around it. Shortly before the fence curves to the right, go up the hill, past two more small ponds.

20. Deer. Deer move around the Park freely, but the area to the side of the Spinney is a favourite spot. It is important not to disturb them by approaching them.

Stay 50 metres from the deer at all times and keep your dog on a lead, however well behaved it is normally.

21. Two New Ponds. These were dug out at the end of 2009. It is extremely muddy here! One pond leads into the other with a little waterfall. In time this will be a lovely spot to watch the wildlife come to find water, although the ponds may dry out in summer.

22. Root Hole. Look for this in the grass, just past the last large beech tree on your left, before you cross the road. The roots of the tree have made a perfect hole for collecting rainwater. This little, stagnant pool is an ideal habitat for some tiny insects.

Turn left and cross the road to the car park.

The Nature Collection

The author Susanna Ramsey has a unique collection of animal bones, feathers, antlers and owl pellets, which she takes into local schools and nurseries. Almost everything in The Nature Collection relates to the wildlife in Richmond Park and many objects have been collected from the Park, with the special permission of The Royal Parks.

The collection gives children and teachers an intimate, 'hands on' experience of the Park's wildlife. Children try on antlers, pick up enormous deer skulls and touch tiny vole bones which have been inside an owl's stomach. They feel how light bird bones are and compare the different shaped beaks.

There are displays of feathers from a tawny owl, little owl and barn owl, kestrel, sparrowhawk, magpie and jay, robin, green and great spotted woodpecker and various ducks. Children use magnifying glasses to examine a wide range of butterflies, moths, bees and beetles. Skeletons include: a fox, frog, grass snake, green woodpecker, shrew, tawny owl, vole and wood mouse.

The Nature Collection can be booked to come to a school or nursery, for a half or full day. As well as showing the collection, Susanna also runs workshops to link the collection in to topics in the National Curriculum, such as Animal Adaptations, Bones, Flight, Food Chains and Habitats.

To learn more about The Nature Collection visit www.thenaturecollection.co.uk

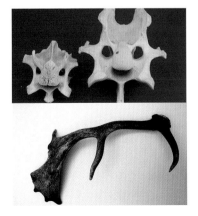

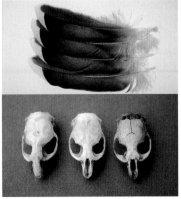

FRIENDS *of* RICHMOND PARK

The Friends of Richmond Park is a registered charity dedicated to the conservation and protection of Richmond Park and its peace and natural beauty, and to advancing public education about the Park. It has more than 1,500 members. The Friends celebrated its 50th anniversary in March 2011.

The Friends has a range of activities, including:

- Up to 25 walks and courses a year on the Park's nature and history.

- Practical conservation work and funding conservation projects.

- Education, including publishing a Guidebook to the Park and holding an annual photography or poetry competition for young people.

- Campaigning on conservation, Park management, planning, traffic and policing issues.

- Volunteering. Friends' volunteers staff the Park Visitor Centre and work on a History Project cataloguing, and making available on the internet, historical material on the Park.

The Friends produce a newsletter three times a year and send a monthly e-mail to members with news on the Park. There is also a Friends website (www.frp.org.uk).

Membership currently costs £6 a year (£10 a year for a household). To join download a form from the website, or collect one from the Visitor Centre.

The Friends' Guide to Richmond Park

A unique guide to a very special place. 136 pages and 300 colour photographs tell the story of the Park's ecology, wildlife, history and buildings. £9.99 from good bookshops.

Richmond Park Facts

Richmond Park is:

  2,350 acres (950 ha) in area and eight miles (13 km) in perimeter
  The largest enclosed urban park in Europe
  A Site of Special Scientific Interest (1992), a National Nature Reserve
  (2000) and a European Special Area of Conservation (2005)
  Eight miles (13 km) from the centre of London

The Park has:

  30 ponds, covering 40 acres (16 ha)
  550 acres (220 ha) of woodland (about a square mile)
  The largest area of acid grassland in London
  11 gates (six for vehicles and pedestrians, five pedestrians only)
  Seven and a half miles (12 km) of bridle path
  Seven car parks, covering 100 acres (40 ha)
  Seven and a half miles (12 km) of the Tamsin Trail
  20 lodges (including Pembroke, White, Holly and Thatched House)
  Two cafes and five refreshment points (some seasonal)
  Nine toilet facilities
  20 notice boards (some have maps also)
  102 litter bins and 44 dog waste bins
  Three (redundant) underground reservoirs

It is home to:

  630 deer (330 Fallow and 300 Red)
  About 130,000 trees (estimates vary), of which 45% are oak
  1,380 veteran trees of 14 species
  1,350 species of beetle (140 scarce or threatened)
  Over 730 species of butterfly and moth (42 scarce or threatened)
  450 species of plants and ferns
  Over 400 species of fungi
  Over 150 species of bees and wasps
  139 species of spiders
  119 species of birds, 57 of which breed in the Park
  9 species of bats (out of 17 in the UK)
  Numerous mammals such as fox, rabbits, shrew, mouse and vole
  Two Shire horses

It is used by:

  2.5 million visitors a year (more than any other of the
  224 National Nature Reserves in the UK)
  8-10 million cars a year; over 90% pass straight through it
  60 species of migrating birds

Useful Information

Opening hours

Richmond Park is open to pedestrians and cyclists 24 hours a day, except during the deer culls in November and February, when the pedestrian gates close at 8pm.

For motor vehicles, the Park opens at 7am in summer and 7.30am in winter, and closes at dusk, which varies from 4pm in November and December to 9pm in June. The opening hours by week are on The Royal Parks or Friends of Richmond Park websites. (www.frp.org.uk)

Information

The Visitor Centre is located outside and to the right of the gates at Pembroke Lodge, and provides help and information on all aspects of the Park, with a wide range of maps and leaflets and various items for sale. All profits from the centre go to conservation projects in the Park. It is staffed by Friends volunteers and is open:

March to October - Friday to Sunday & Bank Holidays, 10am - 4pm.
November to February - Friday to Sunday & Bank Holidays, 10am - 3pm.
The Park Office at Holly Lodge also provides help and information (see below for details).

Eating & drinking

Pembroke Lodge café provides a comprehensive range of food and drink, with public rooms and a terrace looking out over Petersham and the Thames. It is wheelchair accessible and family friendly.
It is open 9am - 5.30pm in summer
9.30am - half an hour before dusk in winter.
Telephone: 020 8940 8207 Its website is www.pembroke-lodge.co.uk.

Roehampton Café serves a range of snacks, drinks and ice creams, with indoor and outdoor seating. Located at Roehampton Gate car park. It is open daily: 9am - 5pm summer
9am - half an hour before dusk in winter.
Telephone: 020 8876 7933.

Refreshment kiosks are also located at Broomfield Hill and Pen Ponds car parks, and outside Pembroke Lodge gates, serving a range of hot and cold snacks and beverages. They are open: 9am - 6pm in summer.

Toilet facilities

Toilet facilities are located at Ham Gate, Petersham Gate, next to the Visitor Centre at Pembroke Lodge, Richmond Gate, Sheen Gate, Roehampton Gate café, Robin Hood Gate, Isabella Plantation and Kingston Gate. All except Ham and Petersham Gates have disabled facilities; at Isabella the disabled toilet is at the lower (northern) gate.

Park Management and Police

The Park management is located at Holly Lodge; the office is open year round from 9am - 4pm, Monday to Friday (closed Bank Holidays).
Telephone: 0300 061 2200
Email: richmond@royalparks.gsi.gov.uk.
The Royal Parks website is www.royalparks.org.uk.

Police: there are two numbers for reporting an incident in Richmond Park to the police.
If it is an **emergency** phone 999. For **non-emergency** phone 0300 123 1212 Both numbers take you through to the Metropolitan Police control centre, which will despatch the police to the incident. There are normally police on duty during Park opening hours 7 days a week.